The Photographer of Wolves

The Photographer of Wolves

John O'Neill

Wolsak and Wynn . Toronto

Copyright © John O'Neill, 1997

All rights reserved. No part of this book may be reproduced or transmitted in any form, by any means, electronic or mechanical, without permission in writing from the publisher, except by a reviewer who may quote brief passages in a review.

Typeset in Gothic Book, printed in Canada by
The Coach House Printing Company, Toronto

Author's photo: Janet O'Neill
Front cover art: Arlene Cassidy
Cover design: Stan Bevington

Some of these poems have appeared previously in *Prairie Fire* and *The Malahat Review*.

The publishers gratefully acknowledge support from The Canada Council for the Arts and The Ontario Arts Council which has made publication of this book possible.

Wolsak and Wynn Publishers Ltd.
Don Mills Post Office Box 316
Don Mills, Ontario, Canada, M3C 2S7

Canadian Cataloguing in Publication Data

O'Neill, John, 1959-
  The Photographer of Wolves

Poems.
ISBN 0-919897-55-X

I. Title.

PS8579.N388P46 1997   C811'.54   C97-930644-2
PR9199.3.O53P46 1997

For my mother and father

CONTENTS

STORY OF SNOW

Story of snow	11
Postscript	26

THE PHOTOGRAPHER OF WOLVES

What the wolf is	29
Wolf and skull	30
Scrawny	31
Ambulance howl	32
Werewolf	33
Wolfhouse	34
Wilderness	35
The photographer of wolves	36
Definition: Wolf	51
Reading wolf	52

A STRANDING

Frail	55
Critical care	57
Dream of life	59
A stranding	60
A tree	73
Illness	75
End of things	76
The clearing	77

STORY OF SNOW

STORY OF SNOW

1
Scarborough looked like farmland then. Or, at least,
the hydrofield behind our apartment
stretched a snowy bed between backyards,
chain-link fences, barbecues cooking
rust. 20 years ago
the wind was arctic and ice
fingered up the thin legs of the towers, sky
and earth wore wires on their skin. We
fell right in and, fast as sparrows, made 20 angels,
strung out in a jagged line, fence to fence.
Not angels, Ronny said, *bats,* strung from their
ratty heels, the ceiling of Markham road.
Ronny always the one to darken things.
In our building, Brimorton 555

the halls were dark, damp fabric,
the insides of drawers,
stairs like drains, echoey
wells for no wishes, just the
coins of hard heels, canes,
occasional avalanche
(running down, right off our
feet on corners). This was fine,
playing inside, all of us orphans,
our parents changed with every door,
their shifting faces like lamps, hung
from peeling brown walls.
We lived in front of doors,
hammered lethal superballs
down corridors to panic
at the end like birds trying

to find some hole, sliver for escape.
And the light outside
entered when a hinge creaked,
door cracked, the sky
guillotined the carpet, we'd
leap to avoid. And did. Mr.
Sheffield said, *if you make any more noise* ...
threatened us with his bathrobe cord,
in pyjamas at 4 in the afternoon.
We got away, outside, erased
the apartment face with daylight, quick
scrub in the snow.

              We'd skid down
the snow hill by the winter pool in
the cardboard skin of a dishwasher or
chest of drawers, pretending we were inside again
and the building slid off the Scarborough bluffs,
coffin to the burning lake. Disaster,
ecstasy. Wishing the world would end
with a bang because we were young and wanted
to live, to die, the whole neighbourhood
go together, huge toxic snow cloud, finally
would put Scarborough on the map
and simultaneously
off it.

2
Half-an-hour from bedroom to
blackboard, from Flintstones for lunch
to vitamins, *real* history — Samuel Hearne,
Cartier, Abraham's Plains — a heavenly way,
breathless and cold, trees dragged
low by fresh wings, forcing the gates
of Saint Richard's Elementary. I

want the world to freeze, not to exhale
as I watch Monica in her mittens, too-
big boots, backpacked like an astronaut,
but *I'm* in orbit. I pretend she's not watching
as I fight up the snow hill in the schoolyard,
kept from flying off by sopping clothes
and fear of the frost fence (I'd hung my
tongue there twice in grade 3). Jimmy

Patterson gets an ice-ball in the ear
(last summer you *went around* with him
for a week) and I'm glad it's not me led
crying past the mob of girls before recess
shuts, his face all red-hot, wet and snowy.
Back to wrestling on the mountain (it grows

bigger with every fall), piled up with
snow and modifiers, verbs or fractions,
whatever I'm having trouble with. All the things
that roll like a snowball into the fight, like the time
Clancy wouldn't lend me his baseball glove,
or Steve his Sherwood, or Mr. Bunt chased me
up the fat rope in gym (*we have all day,*
he said, drumming the medicine ball). Then Lisa

dropped me to go to the party with Ken
(my whole body an ache when they danced,
and I felt, walking home, that my street
was the world, Brimorton a thin
sidewalk planet, school and home
precarious on either end). All judgment packs

into 15 minutes on the expanding hill,
wheezing hill, recess no recess.
Then the slide across the icy lot,
through heavy fire doors to peel off
the winter, jacket and gloves. *Settle down
for history now.* Whose? Not ours, never ours,
we'll have to shape our own lessons from
these days, from 15 minutes' frenzy into

20 years, gone as quickly, but with no order
to return to, no warm classroom, no
construction paper angels strung across
blackboards, or look of Lepage's glue streaked
through Monica's hair when I lean for paint.

No desks in strict and easy rows.

3
The bins plug with winter. Their metal wheels
screech and grip under stubby cold fingers
over concrete, broken glass. We have to move
the empty bin in beneath the garbage chute,
17-storey metal throat. Boxes stack
roof-high by the freight elevator,
dad and Kevin, Ronny and me spend half of
Christmas day breaking them up, stamping them flat,
dreaming about what came out. We ache and
complain, spit *Christmas* as if it's a curse,
dad keeps telling us how lucky we are.

(Last year, the boiler room floods:
thigh-deep in filthy water, we
bale the Titanic down there,
keep the apartment afloat.
With sewage for a shirt, in rubber
boots too small for his feet,
my dad swears, throttles a pipe:
his face a flare on the dark lake. We
laugh, point at him across waves (water,
and his anger), privileged to sneer because
we're made to slosh through muck,
to share our dad's work, to
see what he does
every single day.)

But we were lazy as chairs, most of the time,
every day our father
shovelled us from our beds,
10 and 12 years old and already
slow, cynical, weary with the world.

(Once, we stole the *masterkey* — escaped onto
the apartment roof, crawled to the edge.
We dared each other to climb higher,
up antennae, between bruised clouds, but
stopped, the fear a little scratch in the throat,
wind in the knees. We peered over
the concrete bluff: far below our dad
muscled a garbage bin, alone, slipped and fell
hard on the ice. We heard him groan from
17 floors, felt that scratch again, afraid
to go down (as if he'd seen us through
the awkward twist of his fall). We
holed up on the stairs, except for Ronny,
elder brother too old to hide. He
took dad's curses, put his shoulder to steel,
worked for six hours that Saturday, eased his
place in our shrinking apartment for a while.)

* * *

The snow comes, and doesn't forget.
The snow comes up high, we go through it,
all our lives, it is our lives.

The snow is my father's words,
the snow is my brother,
the snow their argument
in great gusts, or quiet as threads, or coming
sideways or sometimes
seeming to rise from the ground.
The morning is the whole story of snow,
the night was clear and now it's everywhere,
it is the empty well and the well that's full,
the way the houses are enormous,
the way our building is shipwrecked,
the street loses its direction,
the wind is pulled from a drawer,
the clock is always
black numbers on white,
the way the water finds the flaw,
the angels fill in,
the hydropoles and birch trees tick,
the best days are seen from the other side,
the way the bell is distant,
and the person walking away is
tired and thin and taken in by the snow
as if through a door,
the way the hinges creak because
to creak is the sound of winter.

4
I'm afraid of my brother.
I shrink in the opposite bed knowing
last week he put both hands on my neck,
mad because I'd been smart-mouthed, laughed at
the girl he'd brought home, her lipstick
smudge, perfume stink. Mom and dad away.
You little bastard he slurred, the girl just cracked another
beer as Ronny stopped me breathing,
stopped me, a minute, *two*,
beer smell in my face, his
hands like wet cloths.
Get the fuck out he
spit and tossed
Kevin and me five dollars to go to
Cedarbrae Mall. And for a

time that's what my brother was, two hands
on my neck, face as strange as that
woman's, her lipstick making
lips where none were, Ronny's face
scary and old and with a tight tiny mouth
I hadn't seen before. I kept
wanting my words back, my laugh
like a slap, the branches of
blood in Ronny's eyes.

We walked to the store,
Simpson's dressed up for Christmas.
I got sick near cosmetics.
The snow smelled like beer, and I didn't like
winter for three years.

* * *

The snow is never put off,
regular as pain, cold
hands on your shoulders.
I'm learning to sleep near
snow again, after my fall.
Who is to blame? Who made the world
as if snow was inevitable?
What of those who've never
seen it, have it fall through their dreams,
pile up as responsibility?
Coldness would have no shape,
the sky no bite, the wind no animal,
and sleep no pillow, mattress or sheet,
cold no O in it, open mouth, ice-
hole, spot to be filled. No
street that drifts up right
past the roofs of the houses,
their Christmas lights like
stars cramped in ice, or
signal flares beneath the weather.

5
Ronny lost his job, Rustcraft Greeting Cards, February, 1973.
One day he slept in, Kevin and me
bundling for school as dad
dragged him from
the stinking sheets.
*For Christ's sake he's
done it again.*

Ronny had 30 beer bottles under his bed.

Ronny wiped snot on the wall there. Nobody said

alcoholic
until dad took all his clothes that night
and threw them across the drift in
front of our patio, on howling Brimorton.
Ron said nothing, put on his suede shoes,
passed into the hall, paused before
stepping clear. Mom cried and drank

coffee in the kitchen, marked off
the calendar date like a birthday
she wanted to remember. Dad said

the driveway needs doing again
stared out at the angry
snow between us and Tuxedo Court,
wind-tunnel, field, hallway street.

Ron vanished, stopped
breathing: his bedsheets
drifted up at his thin bed's foot until,
two months later, mom
pulled them taut again.

* * *

I wish I could replay the past,
study every detail of the
path my brother walked, where he went.
I imagine his life on the
screen of the grey-white sky above
the schoolyard behind our new house —
I won't let it in, it's a storm always
brewing big and black and strange and far off,
as if increasing to erase the small dark
cloud of its beginning. Truth is,
I was too young to know —
what my father said or didn't say,
what my mother didn't say,
how my sisters looked on as if watching
a boat in distress from the shore.
Anyway, it's about snow:
these drifts and banks, hollows, hills,
blades of ice in parking lots, strip
malls with Christmas lights.
Every winter the memory falls
in flakes building a whole sleep,
like a glacier crushed by its own weight,
with countless rooms, chairs, sofas, beds,
dank carpets, no entrances or exits.

* * *

These fields of snow become
what I will never do.
My brain rustles like October,
a candle blinks behind my face.
The stubble field near the tracks
locks with snow, six feet up
the birch trees. Every knot
stares me down, the whole place
like a firm decision made — it
judges, excludes, my mind a shovel that
can't, that *can't*, too small and soft for the job.
I'll wait for things to change,
things *will* change, spring will come, all the
expectations, dreams will
shrink, cave, melt
until the drains gasp. The mud stink
and broken lawn will be
my transition from failure to summer —
here, enter the dry year —
hot, humid, windy, sleepy with acceptance,
curtains drift through the open window.
But fall wears a pumpkin to my door,
its mouth of pain, stalactite grin,
its candle like an icicle
drips and gathers,
tells me that winter
and the expectations will return.

6
Father lost his place, seven years before
Ronny left — dad
traded in his tweed suit and briefcase, keys,
insurance career without
insurance on his own bad habits,
beer in the back of the company car.
Took a job as a super, or *janitor*
as my school friends laughed. I didn't know
what happened then — like kids do, I sleepwalked
through those years, taking what was given, never
knowing what was put in: until my brothers and me
had to force garbage bins around, hook up empty ones
so the garbage of other lives wouldn't just spill out,
like ours did onto the winter street in 1973.
Dad saw in Ronny
what had happened to him,
his own boredom at work
a kind of unemployment. Once,
fixing an outside lock, he put
a screwdriver right through his palm,
hand so cold he didn't notice until
he stood at the closet, couldn't
unpin his glove. Then, passed out in the doorway,
neither coming nor going, just
went sleeping, between things.

Mom found him there, quiet as a baby, then saw he'd
nailed his fist to the linoleum.

7
This is the night Ronny comes calling,
beer in the bottle of his breath.
He tilts on our slippery porch,
Santa Claus for our 1993. And his feet
go out from under him, like his life did,
snow still falling. Later, I sneak out to
vanish in snowdrifts, drown between waves,
hurl snowballs against the wall of dark,
wear a blue scarf that, years ago, he'd soak,
whip me with. Now, he's the visitor,
unwelcome guest, foe on a snow hill, debt:
he snores on our couch until
other arrangements are made, other
arrangements always being made (he'll be
shunted from family house to house,
a parcel no one wants). Whispered arguments,
words like cold under the door,
our children will hear. *Three days at most*
I say, insist on his resurrection,
while my wife turns over, kisses the wall.
*I don't want him near the kids. And you
better hide the beer.* I get up and
steal bottles from the fridge, stash them
under our bed. Then, restless, watch late-night tv,
the old RCA in the basement.
Snow fills the screen.

POSTSCRIPT

A memory of warmth if not fire,
the small intimacy of brothers
sharing a history — or, at least,
a parents' basement when we
still had a house. Ronny

leans on one arm in his bed,
smokes with his free hand
while frost scratches the window
and the radio plays
Leafs versus Penguins. I'm
half-gone under covers but
strain to listen as if something
will be lost if I leave him. And I do,

Ronny quiet and cool, strong,
alert to whatever might
enter to break the soothing
play-by-play, or my rest,
or himself, sitting up in darkness,
thwacking his red-eyed cigarette when
the ash begins to droop. I long to

wake up, to sleep, and to wake
up to that again.

THE PHOTOGRAPHER OF WOLVES

WHAT THE WOLF IS

What makes you afraid?
                                Put your
hands on the wolf's flanks, or in the neck.
Climb into the warm-mouthed bed,
with winter near. There is a
low hum, ripple-pulse, as if you've
put your ear to the body of a sleeping cat.
This is a wolf, but all slumber and gums.
The teeth have fallen out, sharp stones
by the edge of the path. The wolf used to

forage in winter. Now, climb into its den
and find a chair toppled, table bare.
The wolf is a snowman, bearded friend.
Stare down the blizzard and pray for him,
on the field like the storm's unwilling eye.

What world is this, where the animal
comes to your door? When you're speaking
quietly your lover sees
the shadow of lush fur on the wall.
This is not the wolf, but what you believe.
Or, sleep through the fear, the animal
with its nerves like branches in your face.
Its cruel bones in your back in the skinny bed.

WOLF AND SKULL

A wolf looks at a human skull
by the Takhanne River, Yukon — coughed up,
this Tutchone boy who went missing
in a grizzly's face. The sun falls, the skull blinks.
Now, the wolf pauses, looks, starts,
extends a paw, turns, coughs,
lifts its snout, extends a paw,
turns, coughs, circles
on the pivot of the skull. Then
breaks off, full tilt from the skull's trap.
Because, for a moment, the wolf was

caught in the dead gaze, felt some buzz that
bit its spine, raised its pulse, that said
(the bone translated):
we are alike now, we are both essentially
what we are, no pretence or disguise
in my fleshless, eyeless, speechlessness

and no pretence in the wolf-like wolf,
always itself, so always
like that skull (crude,
clean, unconscious, blank)
and the boy
only close to wolf
when picked to the bone.

SCRAWNY

At least two hundred pounds, he says. *And growing.*
The park warden halves his estimate,
scribbles on the sheet. *Giant wolf*, she laughs
to herself, strides clear of his campsite.
And a wolf, scrawny as a dishcloth,
crosses behind, chokes on her dust.
It has the look of a drawn curtain.

The man is its enemy. The man will trap the sad
wolf and blow his own house down. The wolf will blow itself
up into a hot-air balloon with teeth, then crash
into his dream, burning. The wolf will tuck its tail between
its legs, and the man will say, *brushfire, flashflood.*
The wolf slowly slides, vanishes, slips from the story
as the man grows a canny snout. And he's
talking, telling, saying

it came this close to me
it was this big
closing the gap in his imagination,
tightening the rein of his belief,
gnawing his fear.

Blue-faced, the wolf coughs like a newborn.

AMBULANCE HOWL

The ambulance siren rises
like the howling of wolves — its sound is
shrill of the wilderness,
alarm my mind can't contain.
I'm afraid of its random birth —
who, this time, is being taken away?
Perhaps this is why wolves howl —
in those instants
aware of their own mortality
and letting fear uncoil,
thin metal against the flesh of night.
The hunter carries
his rifle into the sound,
fixes fluid steel as if he's
hunting his own demise.
He would also, if he could, poke
out the ambulance's eyes,
hammer its flat head,
his name backwards across the hood.
Someday he'll be strapped in, driven off,
so he kills wolves
to listen to their howls
go thin and liquify
against the material dark.

WEREWOLF

Man into wolf. What's so frightening?
The wolf life is simple, direct,
without pretence or deceit
and ferocious only when required, tidy as knives.
The wolf is completely
itself, does not stand
outside itself like a stranger
and prey to just one predator:
human.

Much more frightening — wolf into *man*.
Imagine the animal's horror,
its sleek, straight arrow head
suddenly gone
flat, round, fleshy:
and fat, reflective, morose
its once edgy heart. Also,
perversely unpredictable.
But worse than these, most hard —
aware of its own mortality.
This, more awful than any wolf bite
or curse of the moon. Death on its
tail at every instant.

WOLFHOUSE

The white hill is a wolf not moving.
A wind comes up, and the fur on its
feathery spine riles with snow. I am
telling you there are four wolves
on the hill beyond our kitchen window.
They are coming down the hill to our sink.

You have your feet up. You tell me that
you are resting your feet on the ottoman
back of a wolf. *Come in and relax,*
you say. Let the wilderness take hold
as you drift after dinner on the couch
and the radio snarls.

The wolves are keeping us apart.
Wolves in the kitchen, wolves in the den.
We compare wolves, like children with toys.
My heart beats fast, leaves pawprints.
Our front door swings open. The house
fills with the dangerous animal.

WILDERNESS

Once, he threw her halfway across the room.
The coffee table caught her forehead, opened a two-inch gash.
Lucky it wasn't your eye he said. His apology. Then,
he sat with his decaf on the deck, their yard
amidst a tangling grove of spruce. A whitetail
stepped to their pond, nervously drank.

Their house is big, on the end of a large lot,
town's edge. When his family visits, they envy
the wild expanse, but more how the house
keeps it at bay. *I feel so secure in here*
says his sister, her back against
the new storm window. Even his friends
keep to the deck, never venture onto
their chemical lawn.

Beyond our fence, he says, *the world's a dangerous blur,*
while in the bone-clean kitchen
his wife cooks what he wants to eat.

THE PHOTOGRAPHER OF WOLVES

1
It's as if he's moving across
a clearing in his life — tussocks,
stunted spruce, *choke and splatter*, give way to
the open breath of tundra, breathe in, breathe
out, breathe in, breathe out, breathe
out, out, his breath
hardens in sub-arctic air, makes a
perch for jaegers, who pluck the harp of stillness.
His tensions go, ease into flight, though his
camera resembles a cannon, 700
millimetre lens, echoes the Alaska
pipeline, its splintered vein. But he will
focus it on a loose pack of wolves, who are
busy as mice, who bring gifts to one another
(ptarmigan, hare), who circle and circle
within the circle of his lens (frozen
pond, zero, midnight sun). Not for a moment
does he think of home, the automatic advance
whirs and clicks his mind ahead, while his
wife in Toronto dreams of him: a wolf hunt,
deathstand, strange scene where the prey animal
(husband) gives himself up. But what he craves
is stillness, loneliness, *pause*, the wolves'
lives empty and completely purposeful
in the same instant. His camera blinks,
the image held — wolves indistinct,
foggy as ice, but moving irrevocably,
like glaciers, like time.

He wants to watch wolves, forever.

He wants to be a wolf, put his own
anger down to instinct, necessity.
It's as if he's moving across
a clearing in his life, always, the wolf
skin on him, hackle shirt, he enters, keeps
entering.

2
First, the rush-hour traffic, stultification: his car
fused to the freeway crawl. He already
practises fists. Elsewhere, his wife moulds,
fingers curl, her potter's wheel
lifts through clouds, their wolf shapes
beyond the spinning room. He expects her
to be home: she's overtime. By the river,
grey wolves track the rattling caribou.
Soon, she opens their front door,
avoids its accusing eye. He
punches her in the face. Blood
jumps from her nose, she sprawls on ceramic,
tries to swim, he unfastens a chain of *fuckbitchshit*,
the wolves now gone from the scene,
far from his wolf mask, love affair.

I just want some peace, he says.

Grey wolf on the grey winter hill
comprehends briefly, fleetingly,
the man with the camera who
holds himself in his hands, aims himself,
carefully, becomes what he holds,
while the wolf pauses, in no rush,
parked along the sky.

3
I want to climb into him,
like a cave.
But a warm, furry cave, not
cold, dark, stalagmite.
I want to cradle his pale
liquid head as his arms
cradle me, and
his lips speak a lake
that loons still with song,
that loons still.
I'll make the wolf my cave. Come in.
I'm not wrong
about him. I'll
make the wolf what I need
and pull the pelt
tight to my chin,
the dark a lie,
the cold a stranger.
I want to climb into him,
examine
the far rooms, deep rooms,
with a small
light in my hand
like a mystic word, opening doors.
And my body
will be safe, my head
above night,
though I know that
shadows will touch me, sometimes,
the cold air in shirtsleeves,

*cold air in the
body of a man in the body of a wolf,
furry as a garden,
redemptive as a mountain.*

4
He feels that way, can't help it. He can't stop,
he says, must submit to the claw of his nature.
When he photographs wolves
he is exactly like a wolf on the hunt:
focused, grim, irredeemable, with
blinders tough as antlers, forcing his
eyes to straightness. When he pulls his wife up
by the hair he is
exactly like
himself as he photographs wolves — not
outside of himself, but blind, mauled by the moment,
in the teeth of what he's chosen. (Yet the
wolves he shoots are calm, not on the hunt,
remembering themselves
when their mouths
blurred with blood.) But he won't stop,
thinks of his anger as
inevitable, part of who he is,
for worse or better. And afraid of what
he might become if his rage were
excised: dim, mild, toothless. He
hears the pack close in — their claws
click on tiles.

But she, too, considers wolves. They're pale ghosts
on the edge of the lawn, dreamy as moonbeams,
though teeth glint like cutlery. One comes forward,
a bruised, three-legged dog, and she puts her
arms in, as if she can shape it, mould it
into what she wants. Its hot breath rises in fog,
slavers everything.

5
Her friends tell her to leave. But she won't, as if
his exquisite eye, needling craft makes her
pain necessary. She's the wolf he must
sacrifice, exile with his sins like the
beasts of Gevaudan, or the North American timber wolf,
beaten, buckshot, strychnined. *Get counselling*, they advise, talking
slowly: their words halt with import. And she can't hate his art,
although the arctic wolves along their hall, in simple frames,
images of his devotion, are sold to those whose wilderness
is the stillness of the stripped rose, and the animal silhouette.
Not for them the things he's seen, what he *feels*, a moose torn open,
skull like a bowl, the red wolves hotly gorging themselves.
This is the real beauty, he says, the animal absorbed,
in the act completely itself, and not the immaculate
wind-swept wolf, coy on the ridge. She lets him ramble on, again,
his words like run-off, and he goes *don't walk out on me*
as if he's no part of it, and it all begins again, them
going in circles, and she wishing that their life mirrored those
pristine wolves, almost hovering above the hills,
content in themselves, in the shattering cold,
in the bad wolf day.

6
*It's just that I guess
I need to change jobs,* he says. *Too much stress.*
He is the photographer of wolves, and
nothing else. Then leans forward as if
laying his camera down, and closes his eyes
in a kind of kiss. Whispers erotically
if I could quit the magazine, do it full time
while the marriage counsellor tries to keep
her eyes off his wife, her cheek a dark stain.
Well, this is a beginning, the counsellor says,
thinking he won't talk about it
though she knows he carries his own father's
anger like a bone. Then the couple
lock eyes. Between them
a disturbance in the air, a ruffle, sniff,
something stirs invisibly so the counsellor
counsels herself, tugs her skirt tight,
snaps her pen up, afraid. *Let's continue,*
she coughs, and the man stiffens in his chair,
feels his shoulders ache like when the wolf
first appears, steps into his line of sight,
perfect full head shot in his telephoto.

7
*But what have wolves to do
with the homeless man on the curb, Shuter and Jarvis,
clothes shedding him, she says.
What have mountains to do or tundra with this
flaking skin of light,
the smashed glacial pavement? Why hold your lens
away from here, tripod walk
clear of these streets, these blue arms along walls?
What about social relevance?
Why do you photograph wolves?*
This other woman, editor of his book,
tries to steer his gaze onto
the wilderness street, not knowing about his
wilderness life. He always gets
mad when she talks like this: she sees beyond
his photos on the wall.
Now, he rifles through his mind to find some
reason that would let him
breathe (after all, she is *not* his wife). Then, he has it,
lunges for the thought —
*I want to give the
unwanted to a wolf pack,
the unhoused and unwashed to an air-tight
group of wolves, so that hunger
might be learned. What drives the wolves
in my photographs should
infect these men in their
own loose pack around the shelter.*

They pass in an arctic car,
cool air curls inside. *They
are not themselves, these men, like
wolves who've fallen from the hunt,
like dogs and not
wholly completely ravenous beautiful wolves.
I photograph wolves to
teach men to fend for themselves.* He grins, she coughs,
he puts a hand on her knee, anger and desire
for a moment make a paw. She brakes and says,
sharply, stepping free
*but your wolves look friendly as pups. Maybe it's time
your pictures reflected
life on the street. And please don't touch me
like that again.*

8
I'll tell you about my past, about how I came to this,
my temper always set to boil, spill. Well, there
are my mother and dad. They are, what can I say?
Will my biography set things straight, trail
of some twenty years reduce to a phrase in a room,
like a single set of animal prints? I'd rather
tell a story, counsel you: I recall

how a mother wolf put her dangerous
mouth around her pup, and trotted from
where a Yukon grizzly came, swinging his
head from side to side. The pup yelped, but
mom's no panic, white against
rainbow lichen on the hill.
The bear circled,
got a fix on his hunger, then charged.
The wolf fed him a snarl,
plain as bone, her hair
stiff as knives. And that grizzly
skulked away. Oh, yes,

my mother and dad. Why
discuss it? Why slice it open?
Why uncoil the facts
like entrails to read?
When I think of them I've disciplined myself
to focus my mind on this other scene,
to gather the nerve-ends and watch
ten times in a row
that wolf bite down on her young, move
with elegance, and something like love,

bright as the nearby stream
that chatters and speculates.
Then my anger will melt, drain,
like the bear losing itself,
its appetite a malfunction,
its hunger a sin.
I will make my hunger a sin,
my anger a story,
like a wolf.

9
Yonge and Dundas,
6 a.m. June before
the traffic locks.
He looks out from
the greasy spoon, a few
minutes before work
when a wolf might
lope up between buildings,
give birth to itself
in a hundred panes
of glass, smart chorus
line of wolves. Repeat. They are

the first thing in the morning.
In a city that slowly
builds up steam until,
wolf-like, it bares its teeth,
hunts and won't let
go until the whole town
zeroes in on the
kill of 5 o'clock. But less
wolf-like this morning place,
he thinks, chewing
his coffee, where a
yawning wolf might
trot sideways toward Bay,
not stopping for red,
up the yawning street,
rural as a dog.

10
She makes a new wolf,
never having seen wolf track, heard
wolf song. She builds
a nest of his photographs, sketches
and shapes natural history.
Her imagination, patience pushes through
dexterity, precise
fingers press clay into a
swirl of angry
sinew and leg, bolt tail,
teeth on a rumbling chain,
like his final words before she
closed her life behind him.
Now, she works with a meticulous
peregrine look, careful
though clear of the hunt.
When she has
an angry welt of wolf,
smear of intent,
predatory blur,
she palms the plaster mould, pours gorgeous bronze
as if pouring the
spirit of the wolf in.
She makes several before
her pack is complete
ten identical snarling wolves.
But her best is gone, destroyed
her masterpiece:
the wrecked mould.

All that ferocity,
storm and contour around
a still core, empty space —
this closer
to the wolf's nature:
the animal like a rung bell.

DEFINITION: WOLF

Snowdrift, lake.
Arc of a tern, arctic.
The wind around a stone cairn,
through spruce trees,
before the storm. The bolt
axes a tree.
The wolf eye is the tiny
snow swirl in the snowbank,
ring on a finger. Promise.
The way that spring arrives,
ice running off,
the flowers up, cock-eyed.
Summer, with arrows.
Autumn comes, and the wolf
strolls through flames,
tongues of leaves,
a portent of winter.
Wolf. Portent of itself
in another season. Of what we are, finally: strangely
strange.

READING WOLF

Think of yourself, reading this.
You're holding this book,
your hands are working,
you're absorbed, perhaps
thinking about the word
absorbed, is it right? Your mind
runs on two tracks
like a wolf with a river for a spine.
You are reading this, perhaps
annoyed that the poem refers to itself.

You are more than the wolf when you're occupied
because your mind goes off, outside,
a white wolf on a hill that
looks back at itself, sees
the wolf shape of night, and the stars
flow into the sky
on the black river of its howl.

But the wolf is only and ever
completely itself.

A STRANDING

FRAIL

She's thin as our words. A small breeze
would scatter her, or
a truthful voice. Withering
and yellow, she'll soon
gather out of sight. Now, she's
hooked up to the world, intravenous girl,
her dreams pumped in. She is married
to three vinyl bags and a metal pole —
they follow her everywhere.
Her bed drifts up with snow
and she shrinks to a spine, crack
in the winter pavement. Her
thumb-tack eyes
pin her to the headboard.

Her hand is one finger. Her
arm is one finger, her
hospital bracelet
small as a ring — and she's
engaged to be ruined, courting decline,
this girl who looks with
nostalgia at tomorrow.
You can hold her neck like a candle,
faint flicker of her hair,
walk into your future by
the light of her loss.
I feel as if everything
swings from her frail hinge —
the door of this world
contracts and expands,
whispers and breaks,

closes and opens,
and when she dies
there'll be no more
coming or going.

CRITICAL CARE

I watch your
tiny hands that can't grasp,
your mouth that can't speak,
your eyes that can't,
and the food tray across your
chest like a door. Light
from the window drops
yellow coins on your skin.
Your wrists are thin as
the bars of the hospital bed
but they don't break when
the nurse leans across you,
looking down a well (the echo
of your words barely
makes it to the rim). And the easy
sweep of your bed curtain
reminds us that
you can't turn your head. I

lower my voice, place
words as light as leaves —
still, my talk is an affront,
my consciousness a lie,
my vigour in bad taste amidst
your drugged acquiescence:
all the fight in you
drains through the needy
television screen.
She's exhausted your doctor says
in a tone that suggests
you might recover after
a good night's sleep.

So, I try to make myself
smaller than I am, attempt
to mirror your condition,
pretending the fullness
of life doesn't pull me
inexorably towards
the automatic doors.

DREAM OF LIFE

for Patty Ciano

You wake from a dream of life
the intoxication that was
your teenage years —
yesterday in the brash hall,
or Aerosmithed in your room,
or playing bored in class,
though your senses were as raw as
fingernails across the blackboard.
These days are
a million years gone,
you walked in a different body then,
seventeen and your flesh and spirit
one vital thing until
the diagnosis.
Now, leukemia is your name,
the word has taken over who we
think you are, though your mother
won't say it — she keeps you
nameless as if she still
carried you in her womb. You watch
your future narrow to simplicity,
survival your only goal,
and you wave goodbye to your
former notion of time which was
no notion of time,
an adolescent blur. But
your regret is wrong —
your world was meant to be
taken for granted,
and you long for that dream again —
here, where the rest of us live.

A STRANDING

1
Between larger stories on her
squat tv, this midnight
bite of news: a twelve-ton
sperm whale
has grounded near
Long Beach, Vancouver Island.
It's a story of the strange
nature's tic or aberration
or nature not taking
care of its own, throwing
one of its charges onto land as if
some judgment were being fulfilled.
The nameless terrible ocean
as mysterious as nebulae
suddenly
sticks out its scarred tongue
and into the growing indignity
tourists wade like soldiers (though
the news barely touches snug
Ucluelet, Tofino, Port Alberni). Still,
the police cordon off the dying animal
so people won't poke it with sticks and shells
or gouge its flesh for a slice of the
unmanageable sea. The whale
appears to watch: its one clean eye
rolls back then locks
onto the menacing lens.
She remembers all this
as vivid as labour
because on that same night
her telephone

shivered

off her kitchen wall,
intrusive as a bat flown in from the dark —
*mom's in intensive care, she
just collapsed, she looks, I'll
meet you in the lobby in
20 minutes.* She

clicks off the aquarium screen, images of
the ruined whale
drain through the hardwood floor
but linger
with the sense of her brother's voice,
viscous and slow,
curling over at the end of every word,
breaking on the end of her normal day.
Normal. The word feels

odd, now, she tries to
pin it to a dream. She thinks: *I should be
drifting into sleep, at this hour.* Instead she
unpeels her apartment
and in a muscular wind
her umbrella snaps
inside out, ribs
exposed to the rainy city. Soon,
she approaches the neon H,
letter branded on the numinous
body of night. Or on
a land-locked whale,
dressed in fiery windows.

2
Her dry mouth forces a smile until the skin
cracks. Rings tighten on
swollen fingers. Her hair is a crow
that's been run over (and she jokes,
seeing her daughter's shocked face,
my hair needs a separate bed).
She doesn't say
*Amy, the cancer's bad, spread
all through me*, not because
she wants to spare her daughter the truth
but because she believes
she still has a hope, and her words
might hasten the end, might
stamp approval on her decline.
But her body has already
out-distanced her words,
has taken a fatal course
as it did years ago
in a marriage made of
deliberate routine,
then through a sad pregnancy
and months of what her doctor
so easily termed
postpartum blues. Now
she refuses to speak of death
or of anything that might
cast a stout shadow
so she bites hard on her lower lip
and Amy sees that, for over an hour,
the red mark remains.

3
IN THE HOSPITAL, WHAT AMY AND HER MOTHER TALK ABOUT

Cleanliness, weather, nurses, children, Amy's ex-husband Bill, her broken VCR, her daughter Jane's 3-day school suspension, the surliness of the hospital receptionist, Amy's recently divorced next-door neighbour Jack Doyle, weather, how Amy's mother nearly went face-first into her salmon when she collapsed at dinner, the man in the next room suffering from elephantiasis, cleanliness, the perverse proliferation of hospital clocks, Warren's new job with the Harbour Patrol, his mother's allergic reaction to medication, weather, foreign investment in the lower mainland, the deterioration of the Lion's Gate Bridge.

WHAT THEY DON'T TALK ABOUT

Whether Amy and her brother Warren will sell their mother's Kerrisdale house, Amy's ex-husband Bill, why her father wouldn't stay with a fastidious, immovable wife, why the family stopped attending Sunday mass, why Amy abandoned plans to finish her Arts Degree, why her mother weeps when she wakes up in the early morning light but not when she wakes in darkness, how her daughter Jane almost drowned in the New Westminster swimming pool, how Amy's father once built her, out of small pieces of driftwood, an enormous, marvelous doll house, how Amy spent a night with 53-year-old Jack Doyle and that he suddenly said, in the middle of love-making, that he didn't want her to think that this was the beginning of anything, why Jane is still on Ritalin, how Amy's brother said *I'm not surprised* when Amy first told him about her divorce, how Amy's mother's swollen hands resemble starfish, how Amy's ex-husband Bill sends his girlfriend Alicia to pick up Jane every second weekend and that Alicia always looks as if she hasn't slept in days, how Amy always tries to examine Alicia's forearms, how Amy's water broke when she was riding the sky-train, the way the ocean smells of wet rope, why Amy's father stayed as long as he did with a fastidious, immovable wife, why whales strand.

4
What pushes the whale off course? Some torn
internal map, or compass bone
just slightly bent, sending a whole life
fouling into bad water? Maybe
a kind of whale dread, existential
fear like a ghostly squid, all
eyes and tentacles. Perhaps
the dragging of trawlers, or
immutable sound of the ocean's
life, turbid and shrill.
Carcinogens? It doesn't matter:
the whale body is huge,
more awful than cause, derailed
train on the edge of a continent.
All of that flow, swagger,
that essential *whaleness*
a sudden liability, it is
slowly being crushed by its own weight.
Even if it could be towed back into the sea
(the news-anchor explains) it would likely die,
spent and traumatized. Amy thinks: is
the animal aware of its doom, or does it
simply wait for the waves to cradle it back
from the misfortune of land? And does it
only wake to its own demise
when some souvenir seeker pries
a fist-sized tooth from its delicate mouth,
the local pain a fragment
of a larger disease, dorsal
fin of mortality?

5
HER MOTHER'S BLACK THOUGHTS IN THE CRISP WHITE HOSPITAL BED

I wasn't paying attention. I wasn't
awake, all those years. I didn't notice you
much after your father left,
had finished noticing him
even before we were married
before I stole his lanky slow body
into the exacting ritual, shunning of
the marriage bed. I did like the way
he fit me like a pant suit, and
always had our dishes cleared
and squeaking in the double sink,
his peevish foreplay. Until,
over that sink one night,
up to his elbows, he told me he'd
lost interest in himself,
said he had to go journeying. I
winced at the new word, I didn't
like it, I knew it had
travelled from a different mouth.
So I concerned myself with the small,
the particular, the manageable,
scoured cutlery, scrubbed blinds,
cut back the garden to the root,
kept your baby brother
close to me, you'll
never know how much I
put into the spareness of things.

I tried to explain, how I wanted to
swab your ears and bundle you into
the Maytag when you moved back home,
looking like an old ovenmitt, my daughter,
with burns on your arms, I couldn't
hear you when you said
mom, he did this to me,
I only thought
what do you do to
make him so
mad all the time?
Your life has
boiled over, I can't
turn it off,
it's a mother's duty,
I've been judged for
how you turned out,
this disease seems
part of your life not mine,
but you'll walk away,
until Jane grows into
a mask of still water,
her grandmother's face.

6
RIVER

She doesn't think of her life
as an ocean or even
a small lake — rather,
a trembling stream,
withered arm of water from
some source that, distant,
is strange and inconsequential,
useless as memory.
Her life: evaporation. She doesn't
consider its tributaries,
the deepnesses she bore,
and never allowed
her children to see
past the routine, or time's
unsettling pictures — a bathroom
glimpse of her cellulite legs,
or the abandoned workshop
in their basement, rusted
drill-bits and cedar-shards
still poking out from boxes.
Christ oh Christ Amy hears her
mother say in the middle of innocuous
banter about hospital food.
Both her eyes swim, but she continues
a stone conversation, her mother
with her gaze fixed upon
the small hard television,
leaking at the foot of the bed.

7
EVOLUTION

Between her mother in the hospital bed
and that whale, blasted by sand,
Amy lives. She becomes
the analogy, bridge between images — the whale
trapped in the furnace of its flesh
and a single parent whose pain
gives her buoyancy
like a seething, pernicious tide. The daughter
thinks hard on it, might even write it down,
she is trying to distance herself from both images
by drawing parallels between them,
letting the energy carry her,
and unwilling to accept
bleak nature in its course,
the randomness of things.

Cleanliness: her mother's
plain corpse, scallop-
face, and thin,
translucent hands crossed over a collapsed blouse,
she resembles a slim
wedge of water in an elegant trough.
This is it, Amy thinks — my
mother is both
the capacity of water and the
animal contained. And I am
a creature thrown clear,
obliged to adjust to life in
a different element, now,
my evolution abrupt as
a gusty rain, or a telephone call.

8
The animal's body
dissolves in streams
between hot ribs of sand.
Its purple tongue curls
back in its throat. The ocean
barely aches, thin waves
like half-closed eyes.
Spermaceti oil
drips and makes
stalagmites, translucent
sand-castles. They are

burning the dead whale.
Soon, a bulldozer
grunts and piles against
its face. The man inside
is a quick business of arms and legs,
a red scarf keeping his
nose from the mortal stench.
And he can't recognize
the whale's heart, tumbling
before him now,
big as a chest of drawers.

9
SLEEPLESS

Amy remembers herself
on the rocking deck of a tourboat off Tofino in 1985,
halfway between elements
and forming the word in her mouth like the start of
a tentative prayer:

Whale.

A blunt cry.
Whisper. A little hole pushed through
the filmy air with her tongue.
Like the first time she
spoke her own daughter's name above
that unwrinkling baby face.
A conjuring. Now,
her daughter has fully arrived,
stands by her on the creaking deck
and Amy casts a bandaged arm
towards the horizon where
she'd seen the pod, or at least its
set of silvery fins. She
watches her daughter's face, her surprise,
and they're a mirror of astonishment,
and she speaks her name
as the pod's neoprene wheel
finally breaks surface:

Jane.

Her daughter
presses the railing, wants to hug
all the whales together like a big
rubbery pillow, nibble its corners. All this was
years ago, before
her mother
collided with a bed,
and her brother stopped calling.
Now Jane is caught in the current of her teenage years,
bumped and buffeted, barely afloat.

Alone in her condo, Amy thinks:

I'm sleepless.
My bed is solid and dry,
benevolent as driftwood.
But black dorsal fins
and sharp blades of spray
slice the headboard,
send goose-feathers up,
and are gone in an instant
and as I
clutch for a daughter's or a mother's hand,
there is nothing on either
side of the animal wake,
and even Jack sleeps
like a baby right
through it all.

A TREE

as ordinary as
rain in spring
outside my
bedroom window.
Its branches
will bloom, soon,
snow's convalescence
interrupted by flowers —
they glint and sharpen
across the field
to my eye's edge.
But, in my grief, having just returned
from a friend's grave,
the tree is
a provocation,
needle to the heart,
its spray of branches,
its thick trunk
a road
forking into
empty air.
Even its
beauty is compromised:
examine it closely,
look its
knot in the eye —
wrinkles, scabs, scars
and strange
carved names like
inscriptions on headstones.

Its solidity,
toughness is
material for coffins.
I live near a park by the lake
whose precarious
woods are a whole
graveyard to be made,
only their roots honest
in the night of the soil,
growing ever downward.

ILLNESS

It's the wilderness inside me.
The x-ray found the spot,
fever on a chart,
stain on a map,
tumour like a knot of trees on open ground.
Its darkness could spread
the doctor warns, that small
spot increase
to claim the surrounding earth.
And, I think, what strange animal might
live on that shadowy ground,
what flesh of our fear?
There's little you can do, the doctor says,
but go home and tend
to that garden you keep.
I think of the weeds and
tangling trees that press the fence of my yard,
and of how I've sat in sunlight there,
taking pleasure in their wildness,
in their branches like antlers,
and the way the breeze brings
a smell of spring wetness and shade
when the heat is too much.

END OF THINGS

The snow is without feature, no
glint of sunlight, ripple or distinction. It is landscape
after erasure, details
peeled off like a carbon sheet. The wolf
hesitates against it, hesitates
and is taken. Of course,
she is invisible, no
trace of an outline,
fluid stride, no tight muscular
inevitability, and
the hot mist of her last breath is in keeping with the
general anesthesia.
This is what I see from my hospital bed — my
pale skin
absorbed by the enclosing land. As I watch
(while a futile substance spits through my arm,
and a crisp line of nurses
bare their teeth and wring
their hands with compassion)
the hospital goes,
the scrubbed lobby
squeals, and my shaved bed,
sheets and body drift
completely through that
absence of wolf in the snow in the ordinary
end of things.

THE CLEARING

The animal
enters the clearing. Lifts its
left paw, slowly as sunrise.
The whole space
empties in that instant, trees and rocks and
unsuspecting squirrels
flow out as the raised paw opens
a ragged hole for the liquid world. Yet,
this clearing is not a mere
absence of trees,
but is the moment before any intake of breath,
the pause before any journey, any endeavour,
the hesitation that asks,
should I go on?
In that instant
the animal is as tiny as a thread of bone,
vulnerable as an eye,
strange and wild as a newborn child,
and its fear is the inarticulate, momentary
awareness of death,
death the great
wilderness that contains all trees, lakes, oceans, mountains,
animals, seasons,
and all hesitations.